HEINZ

DISTILLED WHITE

VINEGAR®

Over 100 Helpful Household Hints

Christine Halvorson

Publications International, Ltd.

Writer

Christine Halvorson is the author of *100s of Helpful Hints: Practical Uses for Arm & Hammer® Baking Soda* and *The Home Hints Calendar 2000;* she is coauthor of *Amazing Uses for Brand-Name Products* and *Clean & Simple: A Back-to-Basics Approach to Cleaning Your Home.* She is a frequent contributor to *The Old Farmer's Almanac* publications, including *Home Owner's Companion, Gardener's Companion,* and *Good Cook's Companion.* Christine works as a freelance writer from her home in Hancock, New Hampshire.

Illustrations by Bot Roda.

Heinz Vinegar is a registered trademark of H.J. Heinz Company. Used by permission.

Louis Weber, CEO
Publications International, Ltd.
7373 North Cicero Avenue
Lincolnwood, Illinois 60712

Permission is never granted for commercial purposes.

ISBN-13: 978-1-4127-1212-5
ISBN-10: 1-4127-1212-2

Manufactured in China.

8 7 6 5 4 3 2 1

Contents

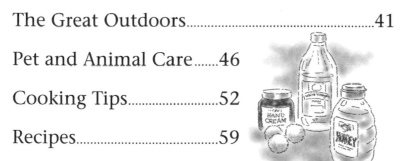

The Power of Vinegar

From cleaning house to preserving food to helping soothe your aches and pains, vinegar can tackle even the toughest jobs. Once you start testing the solutions in this book, you will be amazed by the power of vinegar!

VINEGAR'S VIGOR
In its various forms, vinegar can be a healer, a disinfectant, a preservative, an acid, and a condiment. This list is pretty impressive considering vinegar is a byproduct of something gone bad.

All vinegar starts as alcohol, which is created through the conversion of carbohydrates to sugar. When alcohol ferments, it becomes acetic acid, or vinegar. For example, a bunch of grapes deteriorates to become wine (alcohol), and then wine ferments into wine vinegar.

Vinegar has had its share of curative claims over the years. It was once thought to ward off the Black Plague and prevent scurvy. While these ancient "cures" are dubious, more modern claims are not. Recent medical studies have shown that vinegar can draw venom from a jellyfish sting and soothe a sore throat. It can also be used in the detection of cervical cancer.

SOLUTION AFTER SOLUTION

The following pages offer more than 100 vinegar solutions for cleaning, cooking, preserving, and more. Before you know it, you'll become a vinegar expert. These are a few things you should know before you continue.

Whenever *vinegar* is called for, use **distilled white vinegar.** When other types of vinegar are called for, the specific types are noted.

When a tip or recipe asks you to make a *paste,* mix a dry ingredient with a liquid ingredient to the consistency of toothpaste. Exact measurements aren't necessary.

Fun and interesting facts are listed in the "Vinegar Vignette" boxes.

Chapter 1

Kitchen cleanup

Most people find that the kitchen is the most difficult room in their home to keep clean. And with good reason! With an endless supply of spills, drips, greasy pans, and foot traffic, kitchen cleanup can feel like an endless series of tasks. But thanks to vinegar, you don't need a different commercial cleaner to tackle each problem. An indispensable tool in any kitchen, this ingredient can clean practically anything plus perform some nifty restoration and maintenance tricks.

A+ SOLUTIONS FOR CLEANING APPLIANCES

Coffeemakers, teakettles, and teapots

Buildup in a coffeemaker's brewing system can affect coffee flavor. Get rid of buildup by running 1 brewing cycle of cold water and ¼ cup vinegar. Follow with a cycle of clean water. If you can still smell vinegar, run another cycle using fresh water.

Boil water and ½ cup vinegar in a teakettle for 10 or 15 minutes to help remove any mineral deposits inside the pot and spout. Rinse thoroughly.

Clean a teapot by boiling a 50/50 mixture of vinegar and water for several minutes; let stand for 1 hour. Rinse with water.

Dishwashers

Add ½ cup vinegar to an empty dishwasher and run the rinse cycle. This will open up any clogs in the dishwasher drain lines and deodorize the machine.

Microwaves

If your microwave is spattered with old sauces and greasy buildup, place a glass measuring cup with 1 cup water and ¼ cup vinegar inside microwave. Boil for 3 minutes, then remove measuring cup and wipe inside of oven with a damp sponge.

Ovens

 Twice a year you should "de-grease" the vents of your oven hood. To do this, wipe vents with a sponge and undiluted vinegar, or remove vents and soak them for 15 minutes in 1 cup vinegar and 3 cups water.

 When cleaning your oven, finish the job by using a sponge to wipe entire surface with a mixture of half vinegar and half water. This will help prevent grease buildup.

Refrigerators

 Prevent mildew buildup inside your refrigerator or on its rubber seals by wiping occasionally with a sponge dampened with undiluted vinegar. No need to rinse.

Cleaning Cookware Couldn't Be Easier

Pots and pans

 To prevent egg poachers or double boilers from becoming discolored, add 1 teaspoon vinegar to the boiling water.

MULTIPURPOSE HOME CLEANER

Eliminate the need for several expensive commercial cleaning products from your shelf with the following mixture: 1 teaspoon borax, ½ teaspoon baking soda, 2 teaspoons vinegar, ¼ teaspoon or 1 squirt liquid dish soap, and 2 cups hot water.

Prepare mixture and store it in a clean spray bottle. You might want to recycle an old spray bottle from one of the commercial cleaners, or you can buy brand-new spray bottles at most hardware stores. Make sure you clearly label the bottle and attach a list of ingredients.

Use the cleaner on virtually any surface in your kitchen for daily cleaning. It is especially good for cleaning stovetops and ovens. For caked-on stains on your stovetop, spray on mixture and let sit 15 minutes before wiping surface clean. To clean the inside of your oven, spray on cleaner, leave overnight, and wipe clean.

 Take care of a really greasy frying pan by simmering ¼ inch water and ½ cup vinegar in it for 10 minutes. The lingering oily smell or residue should disappear. Wash as usual.

 Aluminum pans can develop ugly dark stains over time. Remove stains by boiling pans in a large kettle, using 2 tablespoons vinegar and enough water to cover.

Clean the burned-on mess off a broiler pan by adding 2 cups vinegar and ¼ cup sugar to pan while it is still warm. Soak pan for an hour, then clean as usual.

SIMPLY SPARKLING SINKS

Clogs

A mixture of equal parts vinegar, salt, and baking soda may help open up a slow-draining sink. Pour solution down drain; let it sit 1 hour, then pour boiling or very hot tap water down drain.

Clear a minor sink clog with a mixture of ½ cup baking soda and ½ cup vinegar. Let stand 3 hours, then flush with hot water.

Odors

The rubber seal on garbage disposals can retain odors. To deodorize it, remove seal and let it soak in vinegar for 1 hour.

Stains

Tackle mineral deposits around your sink's faucets by squirting them with undiluted vinegar. Let vinegar sit 15 minutes or longer, then scrub away deposits with an old toothbrush.

Clean minor stains in a white porcelain sink with a sprinkling of baking soda and a sponge dampened with vinegar. Stains are best tackled immediately.

For tough or aged stains in a white porcelain sink, cover stained areas with paper towels saturated in household bleach (wear rubber gloves and make sure room is well ventilated). Leave paper towels for ½ hour or until they dry out. Remove towels and rinse area thoroughly. Follow this treatment by cleaning sink with pure vinegar to remove bleach smell.

PUTTING THE SHINE BACK ON KITCHEN SURFACES

Countertops

 Wipe your kitchen countertops with undiluted vinegar once a day to shine them and keep your kitchen smelling fresh.

For everyday cleaning of tile and grout, rub with a little apple cider vinegar on a sponge. This gives off a clean scent and will help cut any greasy buildup.

Wood

A wooden breadbox tends to become sticky with finger-prints and food. Freshen it up by wiping surface with vinegar on a sponge

> ## VINEGAR VIGNETTE
>
> If you pour oil and vinegar into the same vessel, you would call them not friends but opponents.
>
> —Aeschylus

or cloth. Do this periodically to prevent grime buildup. For heavy buildup, try repeated wipes with a sponge dampened with vinegar and sprinkled with salt.

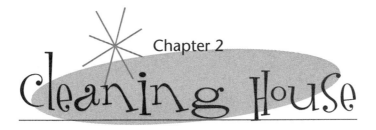

Chapter 2

cleaning House

Are you ready to be astounded by vinegar's power over that grunge in your bathroom? Vinegar is an extraordinary cleaning and deodorizing agent for your entire home. This chapter includes various recipes for homemade cleaning solutions that can hold their own against many of today's commercial products. So stock your cupboard with vinegar, and get ready to tackle your home's toughest cleaning jobs.

Make Your Bathroom Brighter

Bathtubs

A bathtub ring requires a strong solvent. Try soaking paper towels with undiluted vinegar and placing them on the ring. Let towels dry out, then spray with vinegar and scrub with a sponge.

Once a year, dump 1 gallon vinegar into your hot tub, and run it. This will help keep jets from clogging with soap residue.

Showers

Showerheads can get clogged with mineral deposits from your water. Remove deposits by mixing ½ cup vinegar and 1 quart water in a large bowl or bucket. Remove showerhead and soak it in vinegar solution for 15 minutes. For plastic showerheads, soak for 1 hour in a mixture of 1 pint vinegar and 1 pint hot water.

Spot's Stains

To clean up messes made by your pet, first scrape up solids and blot liquids, then clean rug with a rug cleaner. After cleaning, rinse with a mixture of ¼ cup vinegar to 1 cup water to remove all trace of smell and to discourage a repeat performance. Pets are attracted to areas that smell like them, so this is a vital step in your carpet cleaning.

Loosen soap scum on shower doors and walls by spraying them with vinegar. Let dry, then respray to dampen. Wipe clean. If needed, reapply and let sit for several hours. Then dampen and wipe clean again.

Shower curtains or liners can become dulled by soap film or plagued with mildew. Keep vinegar in a spray bottle near shower, and squirt shower curtains once or twice a week. No need to rinse.

Sometimes mildew will leave a stain on shower curtains if not promptly removed. To remove such stains, mix borax with enough vinegar to make a paste, then scrub stained area.

Sinks

Hard-water and mineral deposits around sink and tub faucets can be removed by covering stained area with paper towels soaked in vinegar. Cover and leave on for 1 hour, then wipe with a damp sponge.

Toilets

Pour vinegar into toilet and let sit 30 minutes. Next sprinkle baking soda on a toilet bowl brush and scour any remaining stained areas. Flush.

MAGIC CARPET CLEANERS

 The first rule of carpet cleaning is to wipe up any spill or stain immediately. Often undiluted vinegar can be your best bet for removing a new stain.

 For general cleanup of problem areas on carpets or rugs, use equal parts vinegar and water. Lightly sponge solution into carpet, rinse, and blot dry. Let dry before using area again.

Catsup

 Remove catsup from a rug by sponging a mixture of 1 cup vinegar and 2 cups water into rug. Frequently wring out sponge until stain is gone.

Chewing gum

 To dissolve chewing gum stuck in carpet or any cloth, saturate area with vinegar and let sit briefly. (For faster results, heat vinegar first.) Carefully tug at gum to remove it.

Chocolate

 Chocolate stains can be cleaned with 1 part vinegar and 2 parts water. Sponge on mixture, and blot stain with lots of clean cloths until gone.

DECAL DUTY

Those sunflower decals may have looked cute when you stuck them on the tub to prevent slips and falls, but now they're chipped, stained, and probably out of fashion. To get rid of them, loosen the glue by saturating each decal with vinegar. (Warm vinegar in microwave for about 3 minutes for even better results.) Let vinegar sit for a few minutes, then peel off decals. You should be able to remove any leftover glue with a damp sponge.

Coffee

Coffee spilled on a rug should come out easily with plain water if you attack it immediately. If not, mix 1 part vinegar to 2 parts water, and sponge solution into rug. Blot up any excess, and rinse until brown color is gone.

Cola

Immediately blot a cola spill with paper towels, then clean area with 1 part vinegar to 2 parts water.

Crayon

Remove crayon stains from carpet or any other fabric or surface by scrubbing area with a toothbrush dipped in vinegar.

Glue

A well-dried spot of white school glue can be taken out of a carpet with 1 part vinegar to 2 parts water. Just sponge on mixture and blot. If spot is stubborn, cover it with warm vinegar and let sit for 10 to 15 minutes. When glue has softened, either scrape it up using a dull knife or blot with paper towels.

Ink

An ink stain on a carpet or rug should be treated immediately by blotting and spraying stained area with hair spray. Once ink spot is gone, work a solution of half vinegar, half water into area to remove the sticky spray.

Mildew

Once mildew gets into a rug, it lives and grows. Kill it with a 50/50 mixture of vinegar and water. Make sure rug dries completely. You may want to use a hair dryer set on low to speed drying time.

Red wine

Immediately blot up all moisture from spill, then sprinkle area with salt. Let sit 15 minutes. The salt should absorb any remaining wine in the carpet (turning pink as a result).

Then clean entire area with a mixture of ⅓ cup vinegar and ⅔ cup water.

CARE FOR BARE FLOORS

Ceramic tile

Mop with a mixture of 1 cup vinegar and 1 gallon warm water to make ceramic tile floors sparkle.

Linoleum and vinyl
Scrub a linoleum floor with a mixture of 1 gallon water and 1 cup vinegar. If floor needs a polish after this, use club soda.

Wood
Add a cup of plain vinegar to a gallon bucket of water, and mop lightly onto hardwood floors (do not saturate). No need to rinse. This will keep floors shiny and remove any greasy buildup.

CARPET RINSE

This treatment will help keep your carpet fresh and clean longer between shampoos. Combine ¼ cup vinegar and 1 gallon water, then use solution in a steam-cleaning vacuum after shampooing your carpet to remove any shampoo residue.

Chapter 3

Home Improvement

The chemical properties of vinegar make it useful for many common repair and maintenance jobs around the house. Vinegar keeps painting odors at bay and can remove sticky things like furniture glue, wallpaper paste, and adhesive decals from a variety of surfaces. This ingredient does wonders removing rust and cleaning surfaces to prepare for painting or staining. The list of solutions is endless!

ADVENTURES IN PAINTING AND STAINING

Metal

 Before painting a metal item, wipe surface with a solution of 1 part vinegar to 5 parts water. This cleans the surface and makes peeling less likely.

Galvanized metal should be scoured with vinegar before painting. The acidic qualities of vinegar will clean and degrease the surface and help the paint adhere.

Odors

When applying paint of any kind, keep small dishes of vinegar around the room to absorb paint odors. Keep dishes out for a few days, adding new vinegar each day.

Paintbrushes

Soften hardened paintbrushes by soaking them for an hour in warm vinegar. First boil the vinegar, then pour enough into a container to cover bristles. Do not soak longer than a few hours or bristles may be ruined. Wash brushes afterward in soap and water, then allow to air-dry before using.

Windows

 When removing dried paint on glass windows, first spray the paint with warm vinegar, then carefully scrape or peel off paint.

WALL RECOVERY

Adhesives

 Remove self-adhesive hooks or other sticky accessories from a plaster wall by dripping vinegar behind the base of the accessory. Let vinegar soak in a few minutes, then peel away.

Plaster

 Add ½ teaspoon vinegar to 1 quart patching plastic to extend the amount of time you have to work with the plaster before it hardens.

WOOD REPAIR

Furniture

 If you're trying to take apart a piece of furniture, you can dissolve the old glue by applying warm vinegar to it. Drip vinegar directly onto furniture joints using an eyedropper. Let vinegar soak in, then carefully pry joints apart.

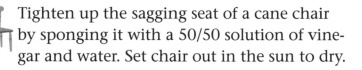 Tighten up the sagging seat of a cane chair by sponging it with a 50/50 solution of vinegar and water. Set chair out in the sun to dry.

Scratches

Combine an equal amount of vinegar and iodine, then apply mixture to a scratch in wood using an artist's paintbrush. If you need a deep color, add a little more iodine; for lighter colors, add more vinegar.

Spots and stains

Use coarse steel wool dipped in mineral spirits to scrub a stain on a wood floor. After scrubbing, wipe with vinegar on a scrubbing sponge. Allow vinegar to penetrate, then repeat and rinse if necessary.

Nuts and Bolts

Rust

Remove rust from nuts, bolts, or nails by placing them in a glass jar, covering them with vinegar, sealing the jar, and letting them sit overnight.

 Rusty tools can be revived in the same manner. Soak them in pure vinegar for several hours, then rub away rust. Change vinegar if it becomes cloudy before rust is softened.

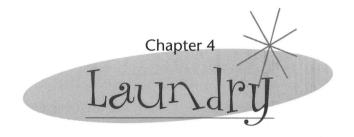

Chapter 4
Laundry

Vinegar is a veritable powerhouse when it comes to pretreating stains, softening water, and boosting regular laundry detergents. When cleaning fabrics, distilled white vinegar is preferred, but apple cider vinegar works just as well if that's what you have on hand. Please note: None of the tips listed here should be tried with dry-clean-only fabrics.

THE BASICS

Blankets

When washing cotton or washable wool blankets, add 2 cups vinegar to last rinse cycle. This will help remove soap and make blankets soft and fluffy.

Clothes softener

Add ½ cup vinegar to the last rinse cycle of your wash to soften clothes.

Lint

Reduce lint buildup and keep pet hair from clinging to clothing by adding vinegar to last rinse cycle.

New clothes

Some new clothes may be treated with a chemical that can be irritating to sensitive skin. Soak new clothing in 1 gallon water with ½ cup vinegar. Rinse, then wash as usual.

TOUGH STAIN REMOVER

Keep this pretreatment solution on hand in the laundry room to use on virtually all tough clothing stains. Just combine ½ cup vinegar, ½ cup ammonia, ½ cup baking soda, 2 squirts liquid soap, and 2 quarts water. Keep solution in a clearly labeled spray bottle.

Static cling

A good way to control static cling is to add ½ cup vinegar to last rinse cycle of your wash.

SPECIAL CARE FOR SPECIAL FABRICS

Delicates

If washing delicate items by hand, follow garment's care instructions, and add 1 or 2 tablespoons vinegar to last rinse to help remove soap residue.

Leather

Clean leather with a mixture of 1 cup boiled linseed oil and 1 cup vinegar. Carefully apply to any spots with a soft cloth. Let dry.

Silk

Dip silks (do not soak) in a mixture of ½ cup mild detergent, 2 tablespoons vinegar, and 2 quarts cold water. Rinse well, then roll in a heavy towel to soak up excess moisture. Iron while still damp.

KEEP COLORS COLORFUL

Any colored clothing item that has become dulled can be brightened by soaking it in 1 gallon warm water and 1 cup vinegar. Follow this with a clear water rinse.

Yellowing

When hand washing linen, wool, or silk, prevent them from yellowing by adding ½ cup vinegar to rinse water.

A GUIDE TO STAIN REMOVAL

Coffee and tea

For coffee or tea stains that have set, soak item in a solution of ⅓ cup vinegar to ⅔ cup water, then hang out in the sun to dry.

Grass

Removal of severe grass stains on white clothes can be helped along by soaking in full-strength vinegar for a half hour before washing.

Gum

If sticky spots remain after removing a piece of gum from clothing, soak spot in vinegar for 10 to 15 minutes. Launder as usual.

RUST-REMOVING TREATMENT

Make a thin paste of vinegar and salt, then spread paste on rust stains in fabric. Lay item out in the sun to bleach it, or apply paste, stretch fabric over a large kettle, and pour boiling water through stained area. In both cases, allow item to dry, then check stain. Run item through rinse cycle in washing machine, then check stain again. Repeat treatment if any stain remains.

Ink

An older ink stain in cotton fabric may be helped by spraying with hair spray. Dab with vinegar to remove sticky spray.

Juice

Dried red berry juice may be removed from bleach-safe garments by soaking in a solution of ⅓ vinegar and ⅔ water. Then wash as usual.

Mildew

A mixture of salt, vinegar, and water should remove mildew stains on most fabrics. Use up to full-strength vinegar if mildew is extensive.

Pretreatment

For synthetic blends or old stains on natural materials, presoak stain in ammonia before applying vinegar and water.

A basic mixture of half water and half vinegar as a laundry pretreatment can do the trick with many common stains on clothing. Keep a spray bottle of this in your laundry room. Spray mixture on stains before washing to give an extra boost.

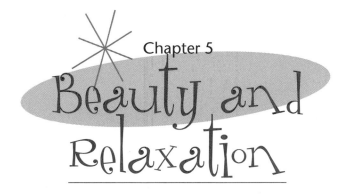

Chapter 5

Beauty and Relaxation

Vinegar is a wonderful—and inexpensive—addition to your beauty and stress-reduction regimens. Vinegar can help restore the natural acidity of your skin, which may clear up skin problems such as dryness, itching, flaking, and acne. Read on for even more beauty tips and tricks that will help you stay relaxed and beautiful without spending a fortune.

Body Beautiful

Age spots

 Vinegar mixed with onion juice may help reduce the appearance of age spots. Mix equal parts onion juice and vinegar, and dab onto age spots. After several weeks of this daily routine, spots should lighten.

Itchy skin

 To relieve itchy skin and/or aching muscles, add 8 ounces apple cider vinegar to a bathtub of warm water. Soak in tub for at least 15 minutes.

Put on a Happy Face

Aftershave

Apple cider vinegar is a great aftershave for men that will help keep their skin soft and young looking. Keep a small bottle of it in the medicine cabinet, and splash on face after shaving.

Cleansers and toners

Use a mixture of half vinegar, half water to clean your face. Then rinse with vinegar diluted with water, and let face air dry to seal in moisture.

Problem skin

Oily skin can be controlled with a mixture of half apple cider vinegar and half cool water. The mixture works as an astringent. You can also freeze this solution into ice cubes and use it as a cooling facial treatment on a hot summer day.

ACNE TREATMENT

Use a clean travel-size bottle to mix 1 teaspoon vinegar and 10 teaspoons water. Clean your face as usual in the morning, then carry this bottle and a few cotton balls with you so you can dab acne spots several times during the day. This solution shouldn't dry out your skin, and the vinegar will help return your skin to a natural pH balance. The treatment may also help prevent future acne outbreaks. Discontinue use if irritation worsens.

Make a paste of honey, wheat flour, and vinegar, then use it to lightly cover a new outbreak of pimples. Keep paste on overnight, and rinse off in the morning. This should accelerate the healing process.

HELP YOUR HANDS

Chapped skin

Mix equal parts vinegar and hand cream to help chapped hands.

Nail polish

 Make your nail polish last longer on your fingers by soaking fingertips for 1 minute in 2 teaspoons vinegar and ½ cup warm water before applying polish.

Scrub

Clean very dirty hands by scrubbing with cornmeal that has been moistened with a little bit of apple cider vinegar. Rinse in cool water, then dry.

HEALTHY HAIR

Conditioning

Vinegar is a great hair conditioner and can improve cleanliness and shine. For simple conditioning, just add 1 tablespoon vinegar to your hair as you rinse it.

Dandruff

Massage full-strength vinegar into your scalp several times a week before shampooing. This can help create healthy hair and control dandruff.

HAIR CONDITIONING TREATMENT

Give your hair a conditioning treatment that will leave it feeling like you've been to an expensive salon.

Mix together 3 eggs, 2 tablespoons olive oil or safflower oil, and 1 teaspoon vinegar, then apply to hair. Cover with a plastic cap, and leave on for a half hour. Shampoo as usual.

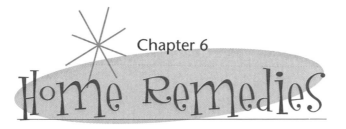

Chapter 6

Home Remedies

Scurvy, cholera, diphtheria, high fever, dysentery, urinary infections, scarlatina, tonsillitis, hoarseness, external inflammations, contusions, joint injuries, apathy, obesity, hay fever, asthma, rashes, food poisoning, heartburn, bad eyesight, brittle nails, bad breath—this is just a sampling of all the ailments for which vinegar has been prescribed. Modern science doesn't endorse all of the traditional uses of vinegar, but this list offers a picture of the seemingly endless healing qualities vinegar may have.

ACHES, PAINS, AND STRAINS

Backaches

 Soaking in a bathtub of hot water and 2 cups vinegar for 30 minutes will help relieve a minor backache and soothe sore muscles.

Bursitis

 Boil 1 cup apple cider vinegar, and add 1 teaspoon cayenne pepper during boil. Cool this mixture, then apply it in a compress to affected area. Make sure cayenne doesn't irritate the skin. The compress should make the area feel warm but not burning.

Headache

 To ease a headache, lie down and apply a compress dipped in a mixture of half warm water and half vinegar to the temples. Also try an herbal vinegar such as lavender to provide aromatic relief.

Leg cramps

Ease the pain of a leg cramp or other cramp in the body by using a soft cloth soaked in full-strength vinegar as a compress.

Muscle sprain

 Apply a poultice of white wine, vinegar, and bran to a recent sprain.

 Use a towel soaked in hot vinegar as a compress to ease the pain of a recent muscle strain or sprain. Apply for 20 minutes at a time. If pain persists, consult a physician.

IT'S FLU SEASON!

Cough

Sprinkle your pillowcase with apple cider vinegar to control nighttime coughing.

Respiratory congestion

To treat head or chest congestion, add ¼ cup vinegar to a vaporizer, and run it for an hour or more.

Sinus congestion

Breathing in steam from a vaporizer can be beneficial in treating the facial

HOMEMADE COUGH SYRUP

During a period of cold or flu, make your own cough syrup to have on hand. Mix ¼ cup honey and ¼ cup apple cider vinegar, and pour into a jar or bottle that can be tightly sealed. Shake well before each use. Take 1 tablespoon every 4 hours. If cough persists for more than a week, see a physician.

pain of a sinus infection. Add ¼ cup vinegar to vaporizer, and breathe in deeply.

Sore throat

 Vinegar can be used for a sore throat. Use 1 teaspoon per 8 ounces of water, and gargle.

When Summer's Not Fun

Bee stings and bug bites

 Use vinegar mixed with cornstarch to make a paste. Apply paste to a bee sting or bug bite, and let dry.

Poison ivy and poison oak

Soothe the rash from poison oak or poison ivy by using a vinegar compress. Mix ½ cup vinegar in a 1-pint container, then add enough water to fill. Chill container in the refrigerator. When cool, dampen a cloth or gauze with solution, and apply to rash.

Sunburn

 Vinegar has a cooling effect on sunburn. Splash it over sunburned area, then lightly rub into skin. Or simply cool sunburn with diluted vinegar in a spray bottle. Spray on affected area.

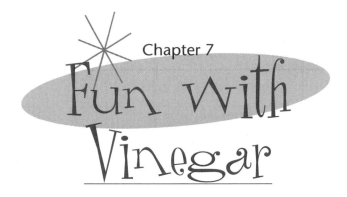

Chapter 7
Fun With Vinegar

Vinegar is an inexpensive ingredient that can be used in many fun arts and crafts projects for children and adults. What's more, vinegar's chemical properties make it an interesting medium for demonstrating some scientific principles. The ideas presented here are only a few of the many exciting activities that are possible with vinegar. Please note: Some of the projects for children require adult supervision.

A Sampling of Science

Make a Motorboat
This easy science project will be boatloads of fun for both you and your children. Be sure to supervise kids during this activity.

> Baking soda
> Several squares of toilet paper
> 1 clean 16-ounce plastic soda bottle with cap
> ¼ cup vinegar
> Bathtub or wading pool full of water

Pour 3 tablespoons baking soda onto a toilet paper square, and fold square into a packet to hold baking soda. Stuff folded toilet paper into soda bottle. You can add 1 or 2 more squares to bottle, but don't overstuff. Hold bottle cap in

VINEGAR VIGNETTE

Some arachnid collectors take great pride in adding a Giant Vinegaroon, a member of the whipscorpion family, to their collection. These 6-inch creatures look pretty nasty, but their main mode of defense is giving off a vinegar-scented acid from one of their glands. The acid won't generally harm people unless they are allergic to it, but a Vinegaroon's pinchers can do some damage. Some people keep them as pets, but you generally won't encounter one by chance because it hides by day and hunts at night. This creepy-looking arachnid is found only in the south and southwestern regions of the United States.

1 hand as you pour ¼ cup vinegar into bottle. Quickly put cap on, and twist once. Put bottle into bathtub or pool. The reaction between the baking soda and the vinegar should cause the bottle to "sail" across the water.

Clean Dirty Pennies

Shine up your pennies, and learn a thing or two about the chemical reaction between vinegar and copper.

> ¼ cup vinegar
> 1 teaspoon salt
> Clear, shallow bowl (not metal)
> 20 very dirty pennies
> Paper towels
> 2 rusty nails

1. Add vinegar and salt to bowl, and stir until salt dissolves. Using your fingers, dip 1 penny halfway into mixture, and hold it there for 10 seconds. What happened? The penny should become shiny. The vinegar removes copper oxide, which is what causes pennies to become dirty.

MAKE MAGIC BEANS

Fill a clear vase with water, and add a little food coloring. Then add ¼ cup vinegar and 3 teaspoons baking soda. Drop in dried beans, buttons, pasta, or rice, and see what they do in the mixture. The small objects should rise to the top, then drop, then rise.

2. Next, put remaining pennies into vinegar mixture. Watch them for a few seconds to see what happens. After 5 minutes, take 10 of the pennies out of the mixture and leave the others in. Put the ones you took out onto a paper towel to dry. Then remove the rest of the pennies, and rinse them under running water; place on a paper towel to dry. Are there differences in the 2 batches of pennies? You should observe that the unrinsed pennies turned blue-green.

3. Now put 2 rusty nails into the vinegar mixture. Make sure one is completely covered in the mixture and the other is leaning against the side of the bowl, only halfway into the mixture. After 10 minutes, look at nails and note differences. One should be completely shiny, and the one dipped halfway should be half shiny and half dull.

ANALYZE ACIDIC REACTIONS

Save a chicken bone from your next chicken dinner, and put it in a clear jar. Fill jar with vinegar, put lid on, and let sit 1 week. Observe what happens to the bone. The bone should become flexible because the vinegar has caused the calcium, which makes bones hard, to dissolve.

Put an egg still in its shell into a jar of vinegar, and check it the next day. What has happened to it? The eggshell, which is made of calcium, should become soft or disintegrate completely.

Chapter 8

The Great
Outdoors

We've already seen hundreds of uses for vinegar
inside your home. Now learn about the many
ways to use this wonderful ingredient outside,
too! Vinegar is a great alternative to toxic chemi-
cals for controlling weeds, pests, and disease in
your yard. For example, vinegar (particularly
apple cider vinegar) is a key ingredient in organic
herbicides and fertilizers. Beyond the garden,
vinegar can work wonders with outdoor maintenance projects.

GREAT GARDENING

Containers

 Remove stains that develop in clay flowerpots by filling them with ⅔ cold water and ⅓ vinegar. Let pots soak until they look clean, then wash with soap and water, and rinse.

Plants

 A squirt of vinegar may help invigorate a plant and make it more resistant to disease and pests. Mix 1 ounce vinegar with 1 gallon compost tea, and use as a regular spray on garden plants.

Roses

Mix 3 tablespoons natural apple cider vinegar in 1 gallon water. Fill garden sprayer with mixture, and spray roses daily to control black spot or other fungal diseases.

Seedlings

 If seedlings begin to mold while starting them in a damp medium, clean them with a solution of 1 part vinegar to 9 parts water, and transfer to a new container. Spritz seeds regularly with this diluted mixture while awaiting germination.

PRESERVING ROSES

Treat fresh-cut roses with extra care by displaying them in sterile vases with a preservative. Instead of a commercial preservative, mix 1 gallon water, 1 tablespoon vinegar, and 1 tablespoon granulated sugar. Flowers in a preservative solution will last about twice as long as those in plain water. You can also extend the lives of your flowers by replacing the water in the container every 2 to 3 days.

Weeds

 Boil 1 quart water, then add 2 tablespoons salt and 5 tablespoons vinegar. While still hot, carefully pour mixture directly onto weeds between cracks on sidewalks and driveways.

PEST PATROL

Ants

 You may be able to stop a troop of ants from marching into your house if you can identify their points of entry and wipe areas with undiluted vinegar. Spray vinegar on thresholds, near sinks, or near appliances where ants are gathering.

Cats

Cats can wreak havoc on your garden by using it as a litter box. Soak wads of newspaper with vinegar, and scatter them in areas where cats have been. The vinegar smell should discourage repeat visits.

Cockroaches

A squirt of pure vinegar from a spray bottle may stop a cockroach long enough to be captured and disposed of properly.

Slugs

Slugs like to feed on gardens primarily at night or on cloudy, damp days. To combat them, fill a spray bottle with half vinegar and half water. Search out slugs at night, and kill them by squirting them directly with solution.

START YOUR SEEDS

You can improve the germination of some vegetable seeds such as okra and asparagus, which are woody and often difficult to start, by rubbing them with coarse sandpaper before planting. Rub seeds between 2 pieces of sandpaper, then soak seeds overnight in a pint of warm water with ½ cup vinegar and a squirt of liquid dish soap. Plant seeds as normal. Use this same method without the sandpaper rub for seeds like nasturtium, parsley, beets, and parsnips.

CAMPING GEAR

Canvas

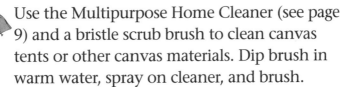

Use the Multipurpose Home Cleaner (see page 9) and a bristle scrub brush to clean canvas tents or other canvas materials. Dip brush in warm water, spray on cleaner, and brush.

If your tent develops mildew, clean problem areas by wiping them with vinegar and letting tent dry in the sun.

Coolers

Picnic jugs and coolers often take on musty or mildew smells. Rinse smelly items with undiluted vinegar, then wash with soap and water to clean thoroughly. Rinse.

Fish

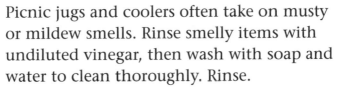

Rub a freshly caught fish with vinegar before cleaning and scaling it. The scaling will be easier, and the vinegar will help control the fishy odor on your hands.

Plastic

Plastic tarps or outdoor equipment coverings can be made antistatic by cleaning them with a solution of 1 tablespoon vinegar to 1 gallon water. This may also reduce the amount of dust attracted to the plastic covering.

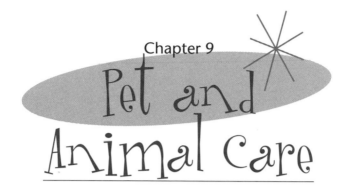

Chapter 9

Pet and Animal Care

You might be surprised to learn that vinegar is a horse's best friend (it controls flies). This chapter also includes several tips for caring for your cats, dogs, rabbits, parrots, and fish. Follow these suggestions, and your pets will thank you!

HOUSEHOLD PETS

Cats

Use vinegar to clean out a kitty litter pan. Remove litter, and pour in ½ inch vinegar. Let vinegar stand 15 minutes. Pour out, and thoroughly dry the pan. Then sprinkle with baking soda, and add fresh kitty litter.

To discourage your cats from walking on, sleeping on, or scratching certain items in your home, lightly sprinkle items with vinegar. The smell will keep cats away.

Control general scratching by regularly wiping your cat or dog's ear area with a cloth dipped in vinegar.

CLEAN STONES FOR AQUARIUMS

You can collect average stones from your backyard and use them in your aquariums, as long as you take some precautions so as not to introduce strange organisms into the water. Test your rocks first by pouring a small amount of vinegar onto their surfaces. If the vinegar fizzes at all, you won't want to use them in your aquarium because they will probably affect the water's pH balance and, therefore, affect the health of your fish.

Add 1 tablespoon apple cider vinegar to your cat or dog's water bowl to improve overall health and digestion.

Clean up urinary accidents from cats or dogs in your home by drying soiled area and then applying undiluted vinegar. The vinegar will help control odor and keep your pet from visiting the area again.

Dogs

Minimize soap residue after a dog's shampoo by adding vinegar to rinsewater. Rinse again with plain water.

After a therapeutic shampoo to treat a skin infection, rinse dog with a solution of 1 part apple cider vinegar to 3 parts water.

Floppy-eared dogs can be prone to yeast infections in their ears, especially after bathing or grooming. To avoid getting water in your dog's ears, plug ears with cotton balls moistened with apple cider vinegar.

Another ear-cleaning remedy is to mix 1 tablespoon vinegar, 1 tablespoon hydrogen peroxide, 1 tablespoon yucca root tea

FISH SNACKS

Some pet fish like to eat the eggs of brine shrimp, but they prefer these eggs to be deshelled. To remove shells from a tablespoon of shrimp eggs, soak eggs for 15 minutes in an inch of water in a jar. Then add an equal amount of bleach to water; stir. When eggs change color from brown to orange, pour them into a shrimp net, and rinse them with water. Fill jar again with water to about ¾ full, and add ¼ inch vinegar. Pour this vinegar water onto the eggs in the net, making sure they all get saturated. Now rinse thoroughly with fresh water, and feed them to your fish.

Something else to feed your fish: vinegar eels! The vinegar eel is a roundworm that likes to live in very acidic conditions—like vinegar. If you're interested in growing them to feed to your fish, just mix 1 part apple cider vinegar to 3 parts water, occasionally add a piece of apple, and your eel will be hatching in no time. They can live for a long time in an aquarium, are a great size for baby fish to eat, and require little attention.

(available at health food stores), 1 drop lavender oil, and ½ cup aloe vera gel. Gently apply to dog or cat's ear with cotton swabs to clean.

If your dog has had a tussle with a skunk, minimize the odor by rinsing his coat with undiluted vinegar. Be sure to keep vinegar out of the dog's eyes during this process. Some skunk smell may remain, but it will be kept under control as it gradually wears off.

If your dog comes home with a swollen nose, most likely he's been stung by a wasp or bee. Make him feel better by bathing the affected area in vinegar.

Rabbits

Use vinegar to clean out rabbit litter boxes and to control buildup of dried urine.

Parrots

Some birdcages are made with galvanized hardware cloth (a type of wire), which can lead to zinc poisoning. This is very harmful to parrots. Decrease the chance of poisoning by wiping the entire cage with vinegar on a cloth before use.

IN THE BARNYARD

Chickens

Use white or apple cider vinegar to clean a chicken's water container. Pour vinegar directly onto a rag and wipe containers, then rinse with water.

Horses

Spruce up a horse's coat by adding ½ cup vinegar to 1 quart water. Use this mixture in a spray bottle to apply to the horse's coat before showing.

Pour ¼ cup apple cider vinegar onto a horse's regular grain feed once a day to deter pesky flies.

Dogs sometimes like to eat horse droppings in the barn. Some dog and horse owners claim that adding ½ cup vinegar to the horse's feed 2 times a day will discourage dogs from doing this.

TREAT WHITE LINE DISEASE

Some horse owners claim that White Line Disease, a fungus that infiltrates a horse's hoof, can be treated with ½ cup white vinegar mixed with 8 cups water and 1 cup copper sulfate. The horse's hooves should be soaked in this solution for 15 minutes for each hoof. Do this at least 5 times a week until the fungus clears.

Chapter 10

Cooking Tips

When it comes to cooking, vinegar has more jobs to do than just appearing as an ingredient in recipes. It can perform miraculous tricks for improving flavor, preserving food, filling in for missing ingredients, and even making food look better. This ingredient can prevent spoilage and salvage the occasional cooking disaster. In fact, if you add a drop here and there during the preparation process, vinegar may change the whole personality of certain foods.

Cooking Tricks

Condiments

When getting to the bottom of a catsup bottle, add a little vinegar and swish it around to make catsup stretch further. This technique will work for other condiments as well.

Dairy products

You can still hard-boil a cracked egg by adding 1 tablespoon vinegar to the boiling water. The vinegar will prevent egg white from running out.

Fish and seafood

Add a tablespoon or more of vinegar when frying or boiling fish to reduce fishy tastes and smells and to keep meat soft.

Give canned shrimp and fish a freshly caught taste by covering it in sherry and adding 2 tablespoons vinegar. Soak for 15 minutes, then prepare as desired.

To keep fish white, soak for 20 minutes in a mixture of 1 quart water and 2 tablespoons vinegar.

Fruits and vegetables

 When cooking fruit on the stovetop, add a spoonful of vinegar to improve flavor.

 When making mashed potatoes, add 1 tablespoon vinegar once you've used enough milk. This will help keep potatoes white. Whip them to desired consistency.

 In a tomato sauce or a tomato-base soup, add 1 or 2 tablespoons vinegar just before completing the cooking process. Flavors will be enhanced.

Meat

 Add zip to a pound of hamburger by adding garlic wine vinegar and ½ teaspoon mustard. Work these ingredients into meat before making into patties.

 Improve the flavor of boiled ham by adding 1 tablespoon vinegar to cooking water.

 The acid content and tangy flavor of vinegar makes it an excellent ingredient in a marinade for meat, poultry, fish, or vegetables. Vinegar can also tenderize tough cuts of meat.

MAKING VINEGAR FROM SCRATCH

Apple cider vinegar

Plain apple cider can easily be made into apple cider vinegar if left to stand in an open bottle for about 5 weeks. The bottle should be kept at 70°F. It will first become hard cider and then vinegar.

Make instant apple cider vinegar by using plain apple cider. Just add brown sugar, molasses, or yeast, and watch it ferment.

Chili vinegar

Put 3 ounces chopped chilies into 1 quart vinegar, and store for 2 weeks in a capped bottle. Strain liquid after 2 weeks. For a spicier, stronger vinegar, let chilies steep longer, to taste.

Cucumber–onion vinegar

Boil 1 pint vinegar, and add 1 teaspoon salt and a dash of white pepper. Add 2 sliced pickling cucumbers and 1 small onion, sliced very thin, to vinegar mixture. Store in a capped glass jar for 5 weeks, then strain. Pour strained liquid into a recycled wine bottle, and cork it. Variation: Leave out onion for a very light vinegar that's excellent on fruit salads.

Garlic vinegar

Peel cloves from 1 large bulb of garlic, and add them to 1 quart vinegar. Steep liquid for 2 weeks, then strain and discard garlic. Use a few drops for flavoring salads, cooked meat, or vegetables. Variation: Use 1 quart red wine vinegar for a resulting vinegar that can be used in place of fresh garlic in most recipes. One teaspoon of the garlic vinegar will be equivalent to a small clove of garlic.

Hot pepper vinegar

Pour 1 pint vinegar into a clean bottle with cap, then add ½ ounce cayenne pepper to it. Let mixture sit for 2 weeks out of direct sunlight. Shake bottle about every other day. After 2 weeks, strain and pour into a separate clean bottle for use.

Baking Tips

Baking soda

Use vinegar to determine if old baking soda is still good enough for baking. Pour 2 tablespoons vinegar in a small dish, and add 1 teaspoon baking soda. Good baking soda should make the vinegar froth significantly.

Bread

Make the crust of homemade bread a nice, golden brown by removing it from the oven shortly before baking time is complete and brushing it with vinegar. Return to oven to finish baking.

You can help homemade bread rise by adding 1 tablespoon vinegar for every 2½ cups flour in the recipe. Reduce other liquids in recipe proportionately.

Meringue

Make a fluffier meringue that is also more stable by adding vinegar to egg whites before beating. For every 3 egg whites in recipe, add ½ teaspoon vinegar.

Pies

Reduce the overly sweet flavor in fruit pies or other desserts by adding a teaspoon of vinegar.

FOOD PRESERVATION

Cheese

Wrap leftover hard cheese in a cloth saturated with vinegar, then store in an airtight container. This will keep cheese from molding or becoming too hard.

Fruits and vegetables

Freshen wilted vegetables such as spinach or lettuce by soaking them in 2 cups water and 1 tablespoon vinegar.

RECIPE SUBSTITUTES

Buttermilk

As a substitute for buttermilk, stir 1 tablespoon vinegar into 1 cup whole milk, and let stand a few minutes. Then measure out the amount called for in the recipe.

Lemons and limes

Vinegar can be used in any recipe calling for lemon or lime juice. Use ½ teaspoon vinegar for each teaspoon of lemon or lime.

Salt

Instead of salt, use vinegar as a seasoning for foods such as potatoes or other vegetables. Just sprinkle on lightly.

Wine

You can substitute vinegar for wine in any recipe if you mix it with water first. Mix a ratio of 1 part vinegar to 3 parts water, then use whatever amount your recipe calls for in place of the wine.

Chapter 11

Recipes

Can you imagine life without vinegar? Many of
our foods wouldn't be quite as flavorful, and
some would spoil before you could even eat
them! Vinegar can add zest to sauces, dressings,
and much more. Read on for just a sampling of
the dozens of recipes that rely on this powerful
ingredient.

Main Dishes

Sauerbraten

    1 boneless beef sirloin tip roast (1¼ pounds)
    3 cups baby carrots
 1½ cups fresh or frozen pearl onions
    ¼ cup raisins
    ½ cup water
    ½ cup red wine vinegar
    1 tablespoon honey
    ½ teaspoon salt
    ½ teaspoon dry mustard
    ½ teaspoon garlic-pepper seasoning
    ¼ teaspoon ground cloves
    ¼ cup crushed crisp gingersnap cookies
        (5 cookies)

Slow Cooker Directions

1. Heat large nonstick skillet over medium heat until hot. Brown roast on all sides; set aside.

2. Place first four ingredients in slow cooker. Combine water, vinegar, honey, salt, mustard, garlic-pepper seasoning, and cloves in large bowl; mix well. Pour mixture over meat and vegetables.

3. Cover and cook on low 4 to 6 hours or until internal temperature reaches 145°F when tested with meat thermometer inserted into thickest part of roast. Transfer roast to cutting board;

cover with foil. Let stand 10 to 15 minutes before slicing. Internal temperature will continue to rise 5° to 10°F during stand time.

4. Remove vegetables with slotted spoon to bowl; cover to keep warm. Stir crushed cookies into sauce mixture in slow cooker. Cover and cook on high 10 to 15 minutes or until sauce thickens. Serve meat and vegetables with sauce.

Makes 5 servings

> **FLAVORFUL BALSAMIC VINEGAR**
>
> Balsamic vinegar, which has a robust flavor already, can make a great salt substitute for flavoring vegetables, fish, meat, or poultry. For additional flavor, add a large pinch of brown sugar per table- spoon of vinegar.

Roast Pork Chops with Apples and Cabbage
    3 teaspoons olive oil, divided
    ½ medium onion, thinly sliced
    1 teaspoon dried thyme leaves
    2 cloves garlic, minced
    4 pork chops, 1 inch thick (6 to 8 ounces each)
       Salt and pepper, to taste
    ¼ cup cider vinegar
    1 tablespoon packed brown sugar
    ¼ teaspoon black pepper
    1 large McIntosh apple, chopped
    ½ (8-ounce) package preshredded coleslaw mix

1. Heat 2 teaspoons oil in large skillet over medium-high heat until hot. Add onion; cook, covered, roughly 4 to 6 minutes or until onion is tender, stirring often. Add thyme and garlic; stir 30 seconds. Transfer to small bowl; set aside.

2. Add remaining 1 teaspoon oil to skillet. Sprinkle pork chops with salt and pepper. Place in skillet; cook 2 minutes per side or until browned. Transfer pork chops to plate. Cover and refrigerate up to 1 day.

3. Remove skillet from heat. Add vinegar, sugar, and ¼ teaspoon pepper; stir to dissolve sugar and scrape cooked bits from skillet. Pour mixture into large bowl. Add onion mixture, apple, and coleslaw mix; do not stir. Cover and refrigerate up to 1 day.

4. Preheat oven to 375°F. Place cabbage mixture in large ovenproof skillet. Heat over medium-high heat; stir until blended and liquid comes to a boil. Lay pork chops on top of cabbage mixture, overlapping to fit. Cover pan; place in oven. Bake 15 minutes or until pork chops are juicy and just barely pink in center.

Makes 4 servings

Note: Instead of making ahead, prepare recipe through step 2 as directed using ovenproof skillet, but do not refrigerate pork chops. Combine vinegar mixture, onion mixture, apple, and cabbage in skillet; bring to a boil and top with pork chops. Complete recipe as directed.

VINEGAR VIGNETTE

In 1842, New York entrepreneur S. R. Mott introduced Mott's apple cider and Mott's vinegar to the commercial markets.

SAUCES

Texas Hot & Tangy BBQ Sauce
    ¼ cup vegetable oil
    2 cups onions, finely chopped
    6 cloves garlic, minced
    2 cups water
    1 can (12 ounces) tomato paste
    1 cup packed brown sugar
    ¾ cup apple cider vinegar
    ½ cup molasses
    ¼ cup Worcestershire sauce
    2 tablespoons jalapeño pepper sauce
    2 teaspoons chili powder
    2 teaspoons ground cumin
    ½ teaspoon ground red pepper

1. Heat oil in large skillet over medium-high heat for 1 minute. Add onions; cook and stir 8 to 10 minutes or until onions begin to brown. Add garlic; cook 2 minutes or until onions are golden.

Add remaining ingredients. Stir with wire whisk until well blended. Reduce heat to medium-low; simmer 15 minutes, stirring occasionally. Cover and remove from heat. Cool 30 minutes.

2. Spoon into 4 labeled, 12-ounce containers. Store refrigerated up to 3 weeks.

Makes 5 to 5½ cups

Chili Sauce
    12 medium-size ripe tomatoes
    1 onion, finely chopped
    1 pepper, finely chopped
    2 cups vinegar
    3 tablespoons sugar
    1 tablespoon salt
    2 teaspoons ground cloves
    2 teaspoons cinnamon
    2 teaspoons allspice
    2 teaspoons grated nutmeg

Peel and slice tomatoes. Put in a preserving kettle with remaining ingredients. Heat gradually to boiling, and cook slowly for 2½ hours.

Makes about 2 quarts